ON THE JOB
Creative Careers

Be a CHEF!

Theresa Emminizer

PowerKiDS press

Published in 2025 by The Rosen Publishing Group, Inc.
2544 Clinton Street, Buffalo, NY 14224

First Edition

Editor: Theresa Emminizer
Book Design: Michael Flynn

Photo Credits: Cover Standret/Shutterstock.com; (series background) KanokpolTokumhnerd/Shutterstock.com; (series boxes) vector illustration/Shutterstock.com; p. 5 Drazen Zigic/Shutterstock.com; p. 7 Anel Alijagic/Shutterstock.com; p. 9 REDPIXEL.PL/Shutterstock.com; p. 11 wavebreakmedia/Shutterstock.com; p. 13 U2M Brand/Shutterstock.com; p. 15 Nancy Kennedy/Shutterstock.com; p. 17 anon_tae/Shutterstock.com; p. 19 Nil Karagoz/Shutterstock.com; p. 21 LightField Studios/Shutterstock.com; p. 22 Krakenimages.com/Shutterstock.com; p. 23 Marian Weyo/Shutterstock.com; p. 25 Jacob Lund/Shutterstock.com; p. 26 Kzenon/Shutterstock.com; p. 27 Mircea Moira/Shutterstock.com; p. 29 Nopphon_1987/Shutterstock.com.

Cataloging-in-Publication Data

Names: Emminizer, Theresa.
Title: Be a chef! / Theresa Emminizer.
Description: Buffalo, NY : PowerKids Press, 2025. | Series: On the job: creative careers | Includes glossary and index.
Identifiers: ISBN 9781499449426 (pbk.) | ISBN 9781499449433 (library bound) | ISBN 9781499449440 (ebook)
Subjects: LCSH: Cooking–Vocational guidance–Juvenile literature. | Cooks–Vocational guidance–Juvenile literature.
Classification: LCC TX652.4 E49 2025 | DDC 641.5023–dc23

Manufactured in the United States of America

CPSIA Compliance Information: Batch #CWPK25. For Further Information contact Rosen Publishing at 1-800-237-9932.

CONTENTS

KITCHEN CREATIVITY

Do you enjoy experimenting in the kitchen? Do you get excited about making meals, or look for new ways to combine flavors? If so, then becoming a chef might be the right career for you! Chefs use their creativity to turn ordinary **ingredients** into delicious dishes.

Becoming a **professional** chef is a very challenging path. It takes **passion**, hard work, and often, many years of training. Chefs need to be imaginative, quick-thinking, and able to lead large teams of people. They work long hours, usually on their feet. But this difficult job is rewarding too. Chefs create art you can eat!

Being a chef is an exciting, hands-on creative career!

CULINARY CAREERS

There are many different **culinary** career paths for chefs. Different training and expertise, or special knowledge, is needed for each.

Caterers make food and drinks for special events. Personal chefs provide cooking services for individuals or families.

Executive chefs (sometimes called chefs de cuisine, or head chefs) work in **restaurants**. They plan menus, create new dishes, and manage other chefs. Executive chefs taste food and review plate presentation before dishes leave the kitchen. Sous chefs work closely with head chefs. They make sure that everyone has what they need to execute, or complete, the executive chef's orders properly.

LEARNING ON THE JOB!

In some restaurants, executive chef is a different position above head or sous chef. Upscale, fine-dining restaurants often have more cooking stations and positions that must be staffed.

Some executive chefs manage multiple kitchens.

STATION CHEFS

Station chefs, or chefs de partie, are responsible for handling certain ingredients or cooking tools. Station chef positions include:

- A pastry chef (pâtissier) prepares pastries, breads, and desserts.
- A sauce chef (saucier) chooses and prepares sauces, gravies, and soups.
- A roast chef (rotisseur) roasts meat. They may also choose the best meats to buy from suppliers, or sellers.
- A fish chef (poissonnier) prepares fish.
- A vegetable chef (entremetier) handles vegetables.
- A grill chef (grillardin) grills food.
- A fry chef (friturier) fries food.
- A pantry chef (garde manger) prepares cold dishes and manages the food that's in cold storage.

LEARNING ON THE JOB!

Junior chefs, called commis chefs, work under station chefs. They measure and prepare ingredients and do basic cooking. Junior chefs may move from one station to another, providing help and learning different skills.

Prepping food and cleaning stations are key parts of making a kitchen run smoothly!

THE BRIGADE SYSTEM

You may have noticed that many chef positions have French names. That's because traditional kitchen positions are based on a French system of organizing workers called the Brigade de Cuisine, or the Brigade System. In this system, workers are ranked so that the chain of command is clear. Work is completed by specialized chefs in an orderly and speedy manner.

In modern restaurants, some of the traditional roles are combined. Kitchen staff is usually ranked from highest to lowest, as shown on page 11.

LEARNING ON THE JOB!

Front-of-house staff are restaurant workers who serve customers. An expediter is responsible for communicating between the front-of-house staff and the kitchen team.

Kitchens are often crowded and noisy. Having a clear chain of command helps keep things organized.

WORKING UP

There are many paths to becoming a successful chef. The most important ingredient is passion! The next is hands-on experience.

Entry-level restaurant jobs include working as a dishwasher, server, or cook. Cooks follow chefs' recipes and meal plans. Cooks have different titles based on their work and experience. Short-order cooks work at fast-food restaurants and diners. They take lots of orders and do basic cooking. Prep cooks cut up ingredients and get them ready for line cooks. Line cooks oversee a kitchen station.

Many chefs start out as cooks. They learn through hands-on experience and work their way up through the ranks as their abilities and knowledge grow.

Many entry-level restaurant jobs require a high school diploma, or level of education.

LEARNING ON THE JOB!

Thomas Keller is an award-winning chef and restauranteur. He's famous for his talent and his very high standards. Keller started out as a dishwasher! Famous chefs Anthony Bourdain and Emeril Lagasse did too.

EDUCATION

In addition to hands-on experience, education can be very helpful to **advance** a chef's career. At a culinary school, students are taught how to plan a menu, use kitchen equipment, or tools, properly, and how to prepare food. Chefs may **pursue** an associate's degree (two years), a bachelor's degree (four years), or a master's degree (two more years) in culinary arts.

There are also special certificate programs which train chefs for particular jobs, such as sous chef or pastry chef. Most certification programs include a certain number of course hours, a written exam, and a practical, or hands-on, exam. Some certifications need to be renewed after a certain number of years.

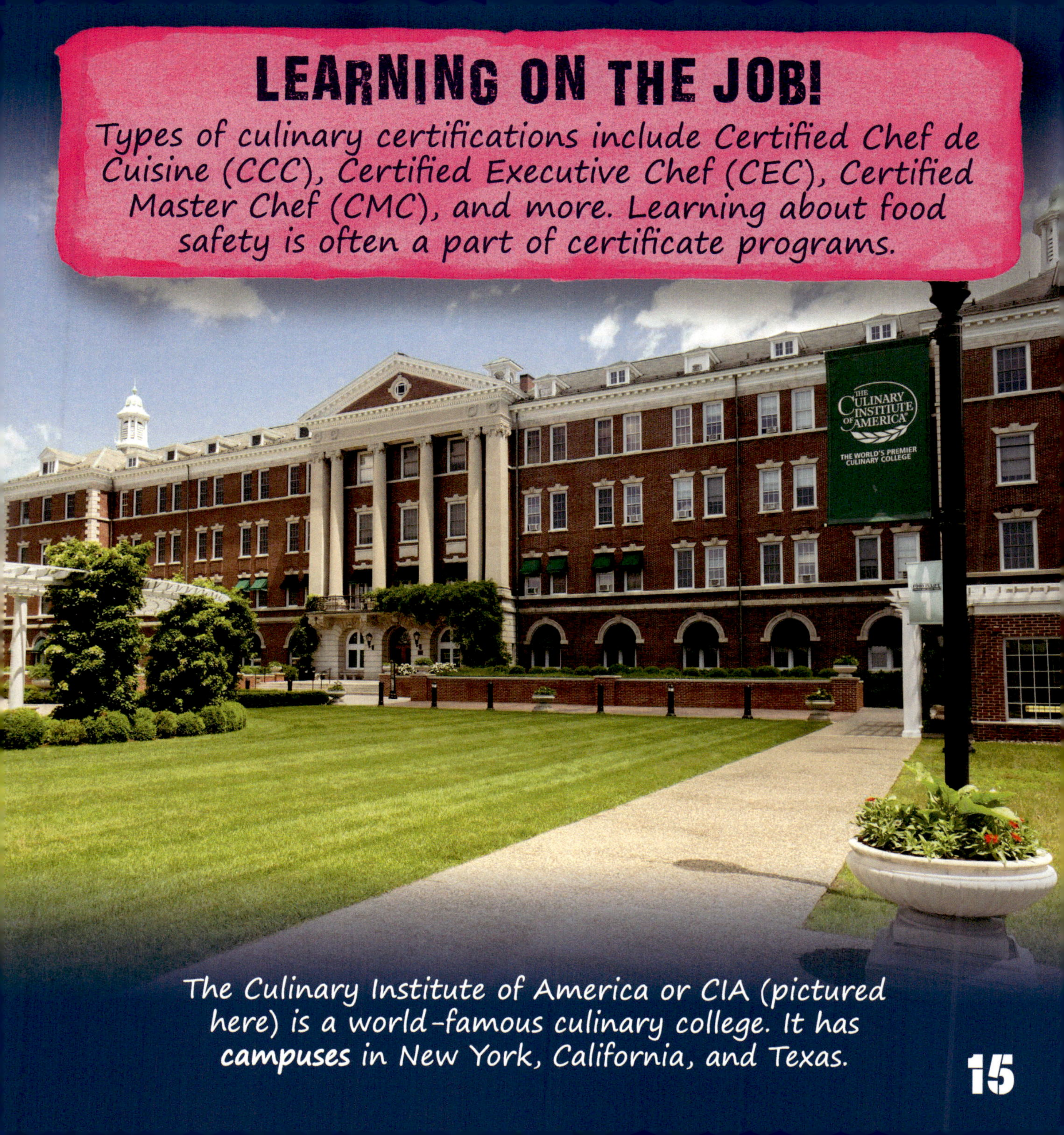

LEARNING ON THE JOB!

Types of culinary certifications include Certified Chef de Cuisine (CCC), Certified Executive Chef (CEC), Certified Master Chef (CMC), and more. Learning about food safety is often a part of certificate programs.

The Culinary Institute of America or CIA (pictured here) is a world-famous culinary college. It has **campuses** in New York, California, and Texas.

APPRENTICESHIPS

Most culinary education programs include an apprenticeship. An apprenticeship is when someone learns a trade, or job, while working under a professional.

Working at a highly respected restaurant or under a well-known chef can be a key part of building a successful culinary career. It gives **aspiring** chefs the chance to ask questions and see how a real high-end kitchen runs. It also allows them to build connections. In the culinary world, having friendships or connections with other chefs is very important. A chef's reputation, or how their character is thought of, can make or break their career.

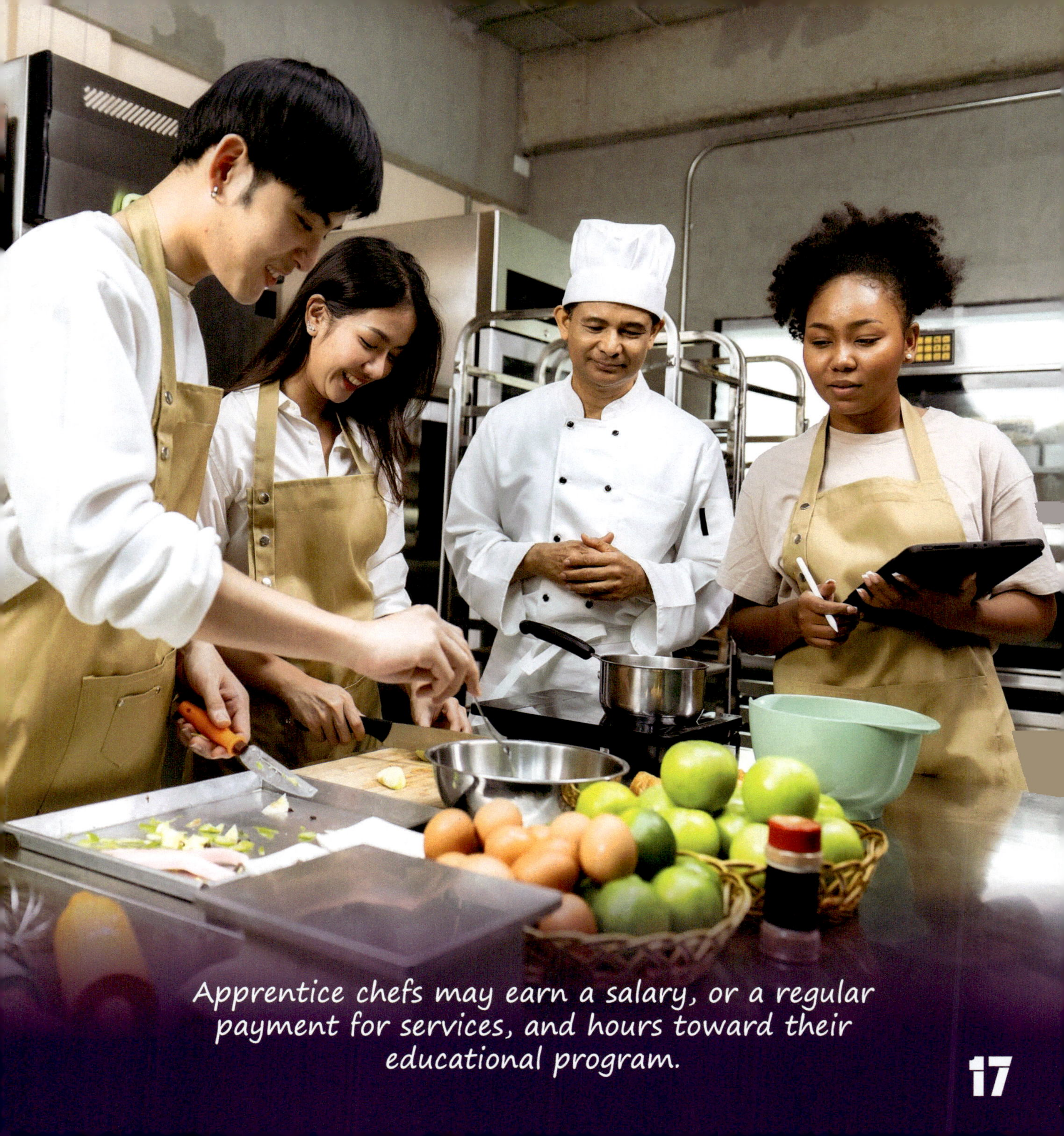

Apprentice chefs may earn a salary, or a regular payment for services, and hours toward their educational program.

SPECIAL SKILLS

In addition to education, certificates, and hands-on experience, chefs need to have special skills. Restaurant kitchens are very fast-paced places, filled with lots of noise and different kinds of people. Chefs are responsible for buying ingredients and equipment, managing **budgets**, hiring kitchen staff, creating dishes and menus, and keeping kitchens safe and clean.

Chefs need to be able to work well with others. They need to communicate clearly with their teammates and with customers. They need to manage their time well. They need to be able to work well under pressure and solve unexpected problems.

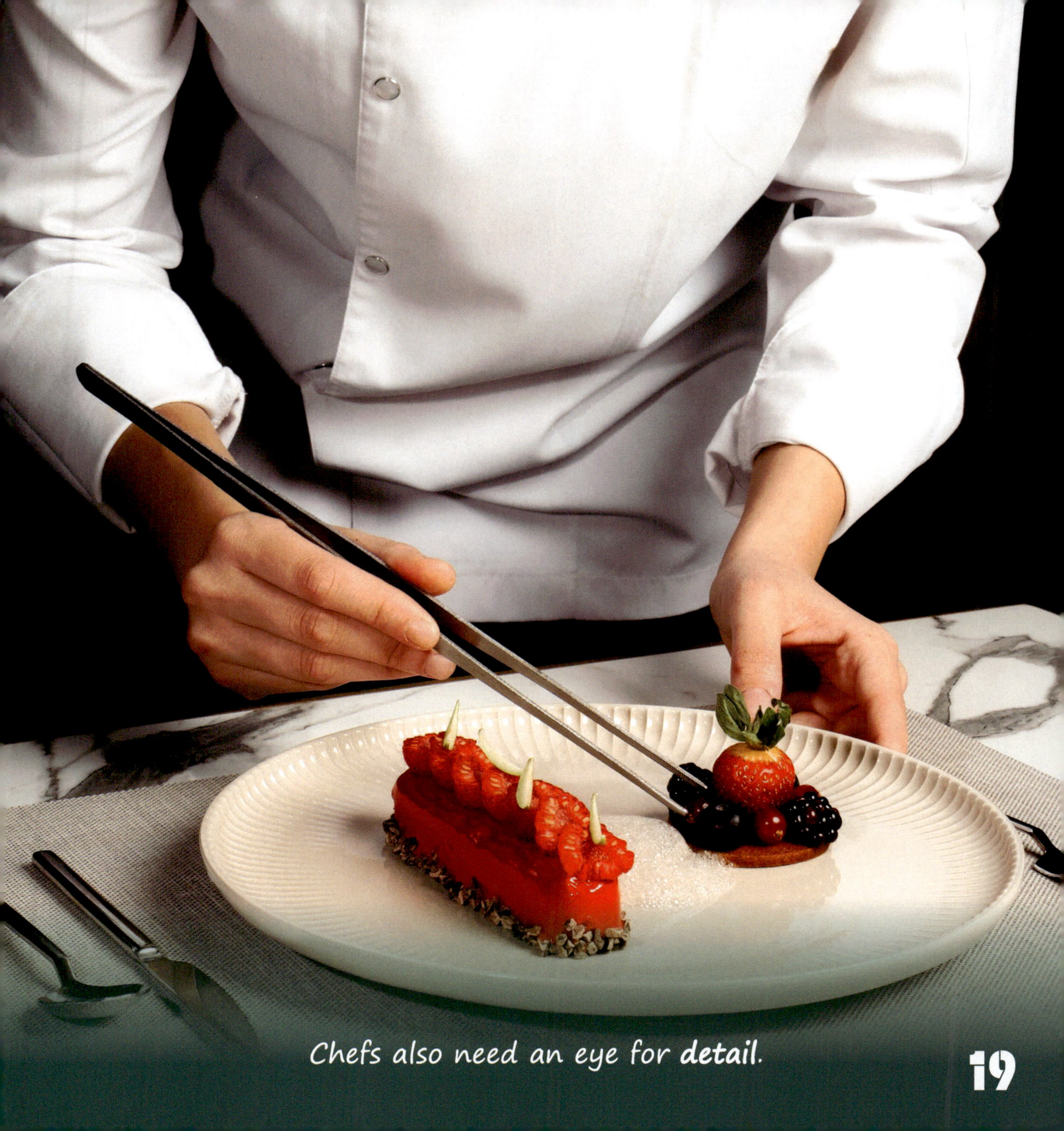

Chefs also need an eye for **detail**.

WORK ENVIRONMENTS

What's it like to work in a professional kitchen? Professional kitchens are busy and filled with many workers. For health and safety, it's very important for kitchens to be kept clean and orderly. Equipment and work stations must be cleaned quickly and tools must be returned to their places so that anyone can find them.

Chefs don't only work in restaurant kitchens. They also work in hotels, food trucks, private homes, and many other places. If they work at a special event such as a wedding, they need to be able to adapt to whatever surrounding they find themselves in.

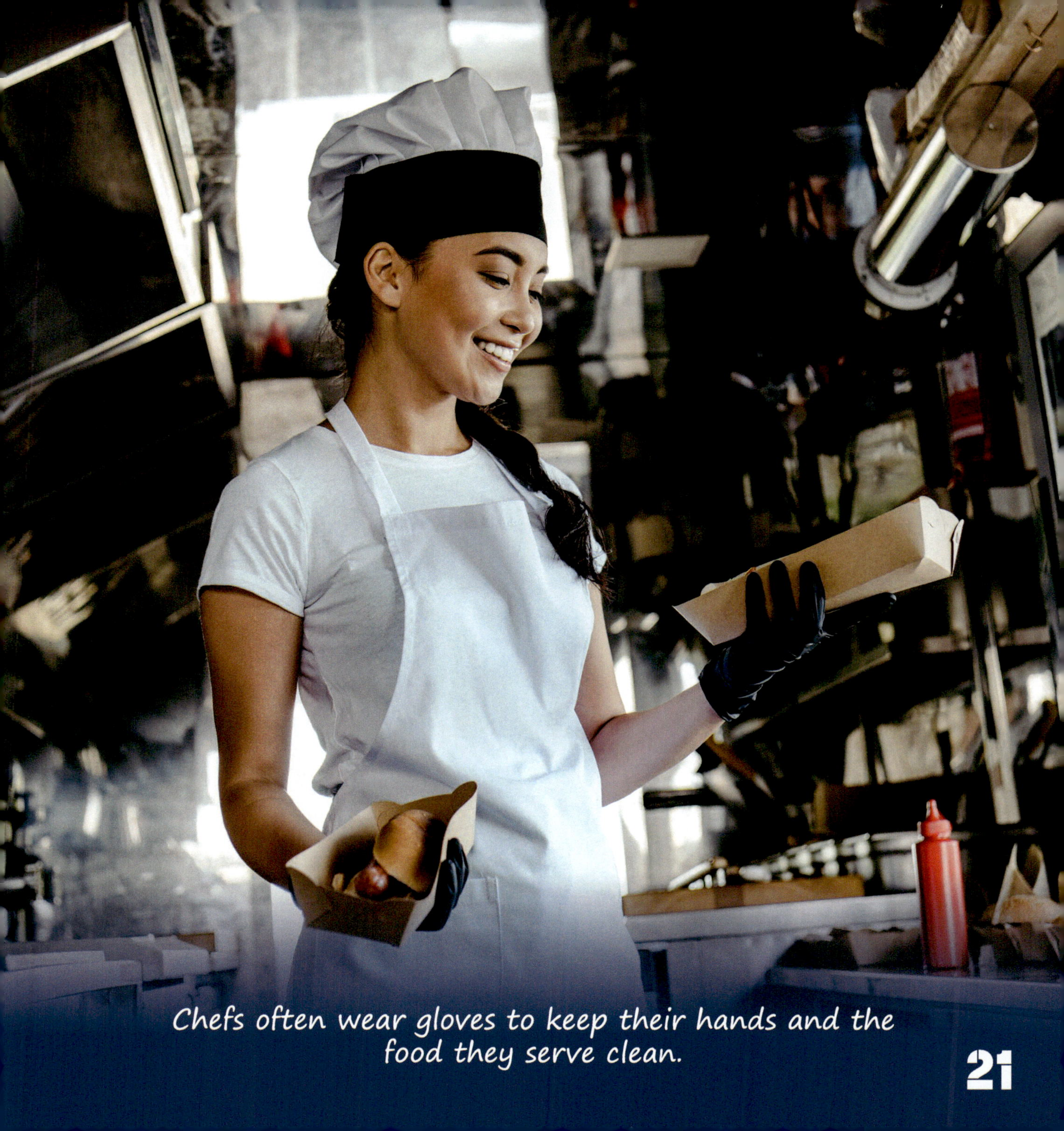

Chefs often wear gloves to keep their hands and the food they serve clean.

SCHEDULE AND LIFESTYLE

Being a chef is more than just a job. It's a lifestyle, or way of life. Executive chefs often work 12-hour days. They are expected to do a lot of planning as well as organizing **inventory** and staff schedules.

Since restaurants are often open six days a week, cooks and chefs work five or six days a week, including weekends. They may work eight hours a day but stay longer than that if there's a rush of customers and cleanup is needed. That means they may work 50 hours or more in a week.

Chefs often come in early to prep the kitchen and stay late to create the next day's menu.

SALARY

What kind of salary can a professional chef expect to earn? It varies, or differs, greatly depending on the restaurant or kitchen they work in. On average, most chefs in the United States earn around $50,000 to $60,000 a year. However, high-end executive chefs can expect to earn around $80,000 a year. More experienced chefs often earn more money.

This chart shows the average income of restaurant kitchen staff listed from lowest to highest.

Job	Average Salary
Dishwasher	$24,000
Line Cook	$35,000
Sauce Chef	$39,700
Junior Chef	$44,500
Sous Chef	$45,000
Pantry Chef	$51,200
Pastry Chef	$56,600
Executive Chef	$61,000

Many chefs hope to open their own restaurant.

PRESTIGE

Beyond salary, there are many reasons why a career as a chef is so appealing. For people who have a passion for food, this career is a way to spend time doing what you love every day. The daily challenges of solving problems and working in a fast-paced, crowded environment can be exciting.

As a chef gains more experience, their artistic abilities grow. They are able to try new things and show their creativity to the world. Prestige means respect and admiration. Being a chef can be a prestigious occupation, or job.

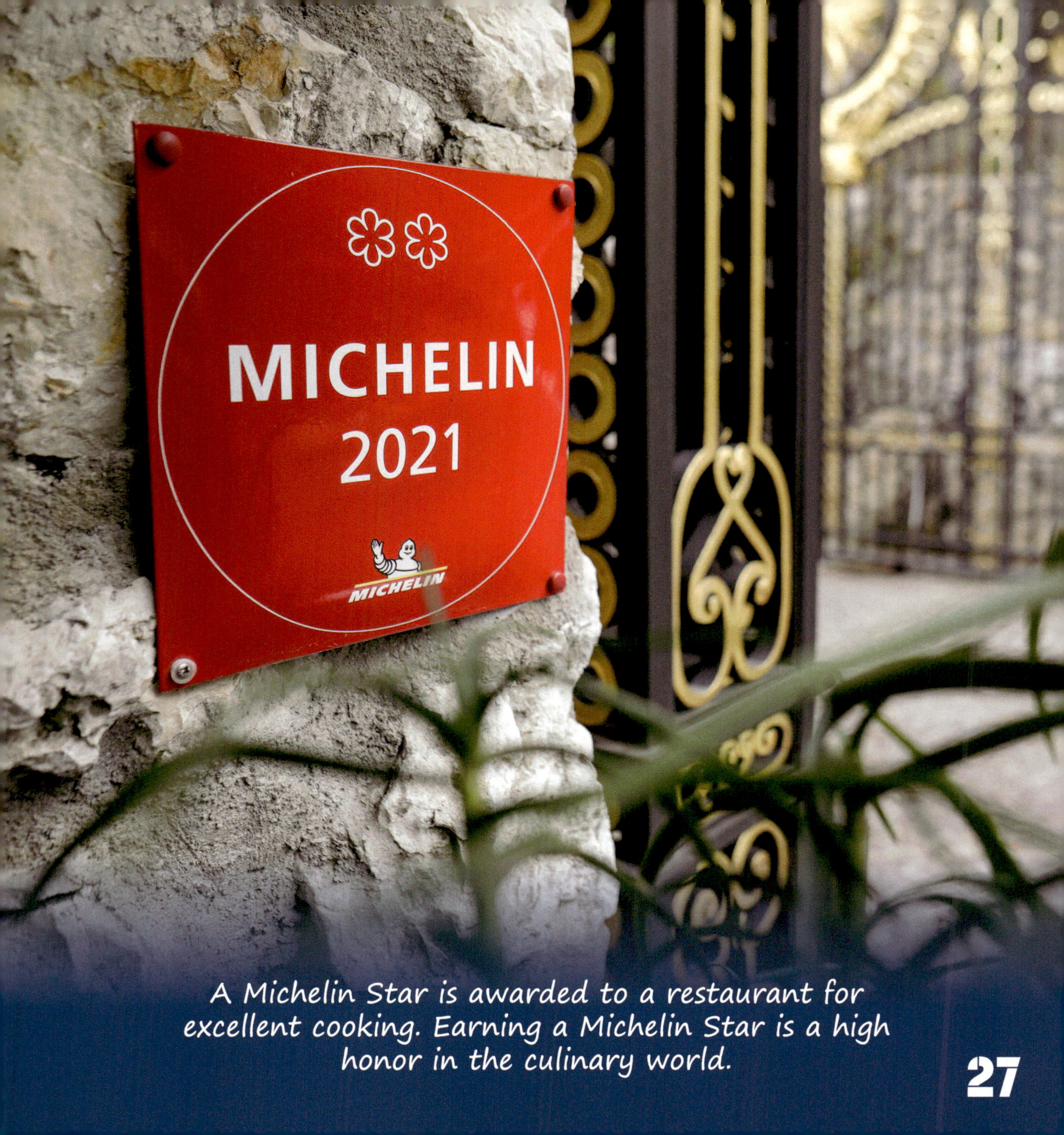

A Michelin Star is awarded to a restaurant for excellent cooking. Earning a Michelin Star is a high honor in the culinary world.

DO YOU WANT TO BE A CHEF?

Picture yourself in a sparkling clean professional kitchen. You have a rich supply of the best ingredients that money can buy. You have a team of workers ready to help execute whatever dish you can imagine. This is a chef's dream!

But to reach that dream, chefs must be willing to work long hours over hot stoves. They must be able to organize inventory, schedule staff, and run the business end of a restaurant. They must spend years of their lives working, learning, and training to get to this point. The best chefs combine hard work and imagination. Do you have what it takes to pursue this creative career? If so, then get cooking!

The number of chef jobs in the United States is expected to grow by 5 percent between 2022 and 2032—that's faster than most other jobs!

GLOSSARY

advance: To move forward.

aspiring: Strongly wanting to achieve a goal.

budget: The amount of money to spend on something.

campus: The grounds and buildings of a university or college.

culinary: Having to do with cooking.

detail: A small part of something.

ingredient: The foods or other components used to make something.

inventory: A supply of goods kept in a certain place.

passion: Enthusiasm or love for something.

professional: Having to do with a certain job someone does for a living.

pursue: To go after something.

restaurant: A place where people buy and eat meals.

FOR MORE INFORMATION

BOOKS

Reeves, Diane Lindsey. *Do You Like Cooking?* Ann Arbor, MI: Cherry Lake Publishing, 2023.

Reeves, Diane Lindsey. *What Chefs Need to Know.* Ann Arbor, MI: Cherry Lake Publishing, 2024.

WEBSITES

Culinary Schools
www.culinaryschools.org/cooking-school-types/kids/future-chefs.php
Try out recipes, learn about kitchen safety, and find out more about becoming a chef on this exciting site!

Wonderopolis
wonderopolis.org/wonder/how-do-you-become-a-chef
Read more helpful tips on how to become a chef.

INDEX